First published 1997

ISBN 0 7110 2520 7

© Ian Allan Ltd 1997

Published by Ian Allan Publishing

an imprint of Ian Allan Ltd, Terminal House, Station Approach,
Shepperton, Surrey TW17 8AS.
Printed by Ian Allan Printing Ltd, at its works at Coombelands in
Runnymede, England.

Code: 9706/2

IAN ALLAN
Publishing

Front Cover: The impressive pairing of two Great
Western 'Manor' class 4-6-0s at work on the West
Somerset Railway. Nos 7820 *Dinmore Manor* and
7828 *Odney Manor* head a special charter working
past Nethercott, between Bishops Lydeard and
Crowcombe, on 13 May 1996. *Mike Goodfield*

Back Cover: The era of the West Country branch
line auto train perfectly recreated. GWR '14xx'
0-4-2T No 1450, with auto trailer No W228W in
tow, passes Castle Hill, near Williton on
22 September 1996. *Don Bishop*

Right: A gleaming S&DJR Class 7F 2-8-0 No 88
(BR No 53808) powers past the site of the former
passing loop at Leigh Bridge, between Stogumber
and Crowcombe Heathfield, with an up train.
Peter Doel

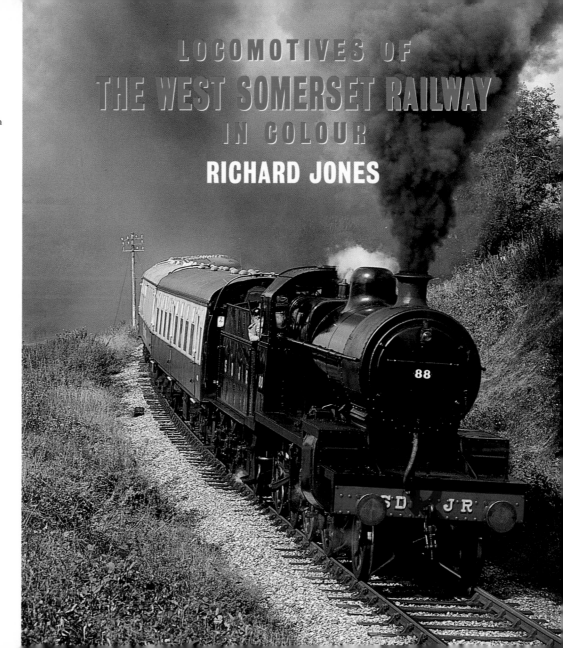

LOCOMOTIVES OF
THE WEST SOMERSET RAILWAY
IN COLOUR
RICHARD JONES

Introduction

The West Somerset Railway, which runs for 20 miles between Minehead and Bishops Lydeard — on which regular passenger trains operate — and a further three miles to connect with the West of England main line at Norton Fitzwarren, near Taunton, is one of the country's most popular and successful independent railways. Running through some of the finest scenery in the West Country, ranging from the coastal plain and beaches of Blue Anchor Bay to the Quantock Hills (see map opposite), the WSR possesses a unique Great Western branch line atmosphere. The Railway carried over 144,000 passengers in 1996.

Built to the designs of Isambard Kingdom Brunel and laid out to his broad gauge, the line was originally built from Norton Fitzwarren to Watchet by the West Somerset Railway Co and opened in March 1862. The line was later extended from Watchet to Minehead, which opened in July 1874, thus giving the line as we know it today. Both sections of the line were worked first by the Bristol & Exeter Railway, and later by the Great Western Railway, and converted to standard gauge in October 1882. British Railways took over responsibility for the line at the start of 1948, when the railways were nationalised. The whole line was closed completely in early January 1971.

Efforts to preserve and reopen the Taunton-Minehead branch started early in the 1970s. The whole line was purchased from BR by Somerset County Council in 1973 and subsequently leased to the new West Somerset Railway Co, actively supported by the West Somerset Railway Association, together with other groups such as the Somerset & Dorset Railway Trust and the Diesel & Electric Preservation Group. Train services were resumed at Easter 1976, when the branch was formally reopened, initially between Minehead and Blue Anchor. Services were progressively extended in stages, the whole line being reopened in June 1979, thus becoming Britain's longest preserved line. As a result, the WSR celebrates its 21st anniversary of operating trains in 1997, and this book has been published to celebrate this important milestone.

Passenger services operate regularly between Minehead and Bishops Lydeard, while the stretch of track between the latter and Norton Fitzwarren is seeing an increasing amount of use, including charter trains from the national network and commercial freight traffic. Over the last 21 years, an impressive variety of locomotives, both steam and diesel, has worked on the WSR.

This book features at least one photograph of *all* the locomotives which have worked a passenger train between Minehead and Bishops Lydeard up to the end of 1996. No less than 49 locomotives are featured. The portfolio of photographs take the reader on a journey along the line starting, literally, at the buffer stops

at Minehead and running through to Bishops Lydeard. They portray the beauty of the scenery along the line — undoubtedly one of the railway's strengths — in all four seasons, and feature a wide variety of locations and trains. No excuse is offered for conveying the impression that the sun always seems to shine in West Somerset!

May the WSR, too, continue to shine in the years ahead...

Acknowledgements

The author offers his sincere thanks to all those whose work appears in these pages, without whose contribution the book would not have been possible. Choosing the photographs to be included, and what to leave out, was undoubtedly the most difficult task of all, such was the very high quality of the material submitted. I am also grateful to John Pearce, whose idea it was to publish the book and who approached me to edit it, and also to the Board of Directors of the West Somerset Railway Association for agreeing to support the project.

Richard Jones
Milverton
Somerset
January 1997

The author pictured at the cab of '9F' class 2-10-0 No 92220.

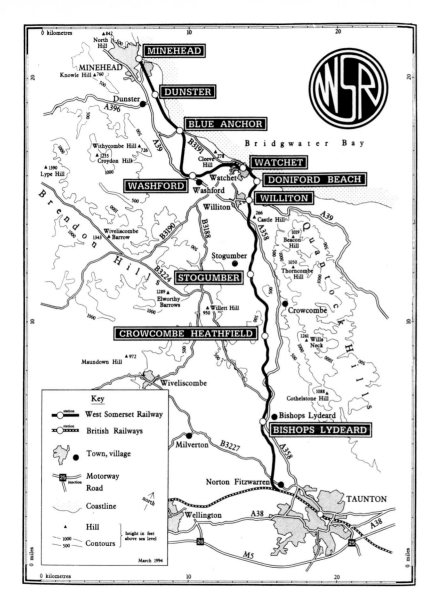

WSR Steam Locomotives: 1975-96

The following is a list of locomotives which have turned a wheel under their own steam on the West Somerset Railway between 1975 and 1996:

No	Locomotive Name	Type	Period on WSR	Mileage on WSR up to 31.12.96
2996	Victor	Bagnall 0-6-0ST	1975-88	24,121e
2994	Vulcan	Bagnall 0-6-0ST	1975-86	25,772e
1163	Whitehead	Peckett 0-4-0ST	1975-78	303*
59	Henbury	Peckett 0-6-0ST	1975-	10e*
6412		GWR 0-6-0PT	1976-	38,430e
53808		S&DJR 7F 2-8-0	1976-	49,303
4561		GWR 2-6-2T	1976-	38,660
1788	Kilmersdon	Peckett 0-4-0ST	1976-	308e*
20	Jennifer	H'll Clarke 0-6-0T	1982-93	2,860
5572		GWR 2-6-2T	1986 & 1987	9,000e
3205		GWR 0-6-0	1987-	21,360e
92220	Evening Star	BR 9F 2-10-0	1989-90	7,200
4160		BR(W) 2-6-2T	1990-	28,638
6106		GWR 2-6-2T	1991 & 1993	7,097
3822		GWR 2-8-0	1992	6,714
3440	City of Truro	GWR 4-4-0	1992	1,128
1	Locomotion	'Replica' 0-4-0	1992	10e*
48773		LMS '8F' 2-8-0	1993	7,688
-	Alfred	Bagnall 0-4-0ST	1993, 1994, 1995	78e*
75069		BR '4MT' 4-6-0	1994	7,308
7802	Bradley Manor	GWR 4-6-0	1994	3,840
7828	Odney Manor	BR(W) 4-6-0	1995-96	11,213
71000	Duke of Glo'ster	BR '8P' 4-6-2	1995	1,059
7820	Dinmore Manor	BR(W) 4-6-0	1995-	13,322
70000	Britannia	BR '7MT' 4-6-2	1996	126
44422		LMS '4F' 0-6-0	1996	1,863
73096		BR '5MT' 4-6-0	1996	266
34105	Swanage	SR 4-6-2	1996	290
34039	Boscastle	SR 4-6-2	1996	660
4277		GWR 2-8-0T	1996	5,734
(1)	Thomas	Hunslet 0-6-0T	1996	10e*
1450		GWR 0-4-2T	1996	649
TOTAL: 32 locomotives				**TOTAL: 315,020e miles**

NB. All the locomotives listed have worked a passenger train between Minehead and Bishops Lydeard except those indicated by as asterisk (*).

e = estimated total

At rest

Two views which show the four engines that were the mainstay of steam-hauled passenger services in the 'early days' of the WSR, when locomotives of industrial origin predominated.

Top left: GWR '64xx' 0-6-0PT No 6412 and Bagnall 0-6-0ST No 2994 *Vulcan* stand adjacent to the buffer stops at Minehead station, literally the end of the line. The latter was one of two locomotives bought by the WSR Co in 1975 from the Austin Motor Co at Longbridge, near Birmingham, whilst the pannier tank was purchased by the WSRA in 1976. *Christopher van den Arend*

Bottom left: Hudswell Clarke 0-6-0T No 20 *Jennifer* and Bagnall 0-6-0ST No 2996 *Victor* are pictured on shed at Minehead in 1983. The latter was the second of the two sister locomotives bought from Longbridge, and the first engine to steam on the 'preserved' WSR. *Jennifer* came to the WSR in 1982, but worked less than 3,000 miles on the WSR. Both engines have now departed from the line. *Richard Jones Collection*

Nocturnal splendour

Right: A very impressive study of SR unrebuilt 'West Country' 4-6-2 No 34105 *Swanage* shows the locomotive at Minehead on 9 March 1996, prior to working the return leg of an evening special to Bishops Lydeard. Normally based on the Mid-Hants Railway, *Swanage* was one of four engines which visited the WSR in March 1996 to appear in a 'Somerset & Dorset Anniversary Gala Weekend' to commemorate the 30th anniversary of the closure of that much loved line. No 34105 ran a total of 290 miles during its brief stay in Somerset. *John P. Robinson*

Minehead departure

Left: With the distinctive profile of North Hill as a backdrop, BR Class 33 diesel-electric No D6535 (later No 33116) *Hertfordshire Railtours* awaits departure from Minehead with the return leg of the 'Ocean Liner Express' to London Waterloo on 5 March 1995. With a very well turned out rake of six green coaches in tow, No D6535 worked the special train throughout, and in doing so became the first 'Crompton' to traverse the Minehead branch. No D6535 is one of four visiting diesel locomotives to have achieved the grand total of 46 miles (one round trip) on the WSR! *Glen Batten*

Matching pairs at Minehead

Bottom left: Two blue-liveried Class 04 diesel shunters, Nos D2133 and D2271, which have been based on the WSR since 1996 and 1982 respectively. Both are normally used for shunting duties at Minehead, but No D2271 has seen very occasional use on passenger services, notably at the Railway's early Diesel Gala events. *David J. Williams*

Below: A pair of green-liveried Class 14 0-6-0 diesel-hydraulics, Nos D9526 and D9551, stand outside the former goods shed at Minehead in September 1985. Originally designed for light branch line work, the Class 14s are used regularly on a variety of workings on the WSR. The building is now used as the railway's main workshop. *Richard Jones*

Popular pannier

Right: In lovely early evening light, GWR '64xx' 0-6-0PT No 6412 approaches Dunster station with the 7.30pm Minehead-Bishops Lydeard dining train on 2 May 1992. The pannier tank was purchased by the WSR Association and arrived on the line (under its own steam from Paignton) in time to work trains at the formal reopening of the WSR at Easter 1976. No 6412 has been a regular and popular performer on the line since then, returning to service in 1997 after an extensive overhaul, its second whilst in WSRA ownership. *John P. Robinson*

Gala goods

Right: Visiting GWR '61xx' 2-6-2T No 6106 heads a Williton-Minehead demonstration goods train away from Dunster station on 5 September 1991, during the Railway's Gala Week. Owned by the Great Western Society and normally based at Didcot, No 6106 has made two visits to the WSR. The 'Large Prairie' was the main 'guest' engine for the 1991 season, and it was hired for a second time in May 1993 to supplement the steam locomotive fleet. Taunton shed had a small fleet of '61xxs' tanks in the late 1950s and early 1960s which were used on the Minehead branch. *John P. Robinson*

Dunster arrival

Left: A superbly turned out GWR 4-4-0 No 3440
City of Truro coasts into the platform at Dunster
station on 21 July 1992 with the 12.20pm Bishops
Lydeard-Minehead service. Part of the National
Collection and normally based at York, No 3440
spent a short period on the WSR in the summer of
1992 in connection with the 'Taunton 150'
celebrations. *City of Truro* — reputedly the first
locomotive ever to have achieved a speed exceeding
100mph — ran a total mileage of 1,168 during its
stay in Somerset, its use being restricted because at
the time the locomotive's axle weight exceeded the
maximum permitted on the line. *Bryan Hicks*

Bulleid power

Right: Evoking memories of the Somerset & Dorset
line in the late 1950s and early 1960s, SR rebuilt
Bulleid 'Pacific' No 34039 *Boscastle* steams across
Ker Moor, between Dunster and Blue Anchor, in
the early morning of 1 April 1996 with a special
charter. Dunster Castle can be seen in the
background to the left of the locomotive. Normally
based on the Great Central Railway, *Boscastle* was
hired by the WSR to take part in the 'Somerset &
Dorset Anniversary Gala Weekend' in March 1996.
Don Bishop

Silver Jubilee I

Left: The principal 'guest' engine for the 1993 season was LMS Class 8F 2-8-0 No 48773, which is normally resident on the Severn Valley Railway. The locomotive is here seen coasting across Ker Moor on the approach to Blue Anchor with the return leg of 'The Silver Jubilee' railtour on 18 September 1993 (4.40pm ex-Minehead), which it worked as far as Bishops Lydeard, the train continuing from there behind a BR Class 37 diesel-electric. The train was organised by No 48773's owners, the Stanier 8F Locomotive Society, to mark the 25th anniversary of the society's purchase of the engine. No 48773 enjoyed a very successful season on the WSR, its power being well suited to the line's steep gradients. *David J. Williams*

Silver Jubilee II

Right: With Blue Anchor station in the distance, 'Hymek' Type 3 diesel-hydraulic No D7017 — resplendent in early BR two-tone green livery — heads 'The Hymek Silver Jubilee' railtour across Ker Moor on 26 September 1987, to commemorate the 25th anniversary since the class was introduced on British Railways. Part of Blue Anchor Bay can be glimpsed to the left of the locomotive. No D7017 was purchased by the Diesel & Electric Preservation Group back in 1975 and arrived on the line early the following year, and since then has been a regular performer on WSR trains. *Brian Dean*

A WSR 'first'

Left: The double-headed combination of WR 4-6-0 No 7820 *Dinmore Manor* and BR Standard 4-6-2 No 70000 *Britannia* make an impressive sight as they pass Blue Anchor's up distant signal and head for Minehead with the outward run of the 'Western Star' charter on 2 March 1996. The train was steam-hauled by *Britannia* throughout, No 7820 being attached at Bishops Lydeard, and was the first steam-hauled through train from London Paddington to Minehead for over 30 years.

Britannia spent a two-week period stabled on the WSR, but worked service trains on only one day, before departing later the same month to resume its main line commitments. *Dinmore Manor* — the first of the batch of 10 'Manors' built by British Railways in 1950 to a Great Western design — entered service on the WSR in September 1995 after an extensive restoration from scrapyard condition, and is now a regular member of the 'home fleet'. *Peter Doel*

Star turn

Above: BR Class 9F No 92220 *Evening Star* — the very last steam locomotive built by British Railways, at Swindon in 1960 — enters the picturesque station of Blue Anchor on 5 September 1989 with the 2.15pm Minehead-Bishops Lydeard train. Part of the National Collection, No 92220 enjoyed a very successful season on the line in 1989, running 7,200 miles, and was a key factor in taking the WSR up to the 'top flight' of preserved railways. *Bryan Hicks*

13

A pair of 'Cromptons'

Above: 'The Quantock Crompton' railtour of 24 August 1996 brought a pair of the few remaining Sulzer Type 3 (Class 33) diesel-electrics to the WSR, following in the footsteps of No D6535 (see page 6). The Civil Engineers-liveried combination of Nos 33208 and 33202 *The Burma Star* enters the down platform at Blue Anchor with the 12-coach train, which originated at London Paddington. The two Class 33s, like No D6535 before them, ran a total of 46 miles on the WSR. The building on the right — the former down side waiting room — is now the home of Blue Anchor Railway Museum, featuring a wide variety of exhibits of GWR and local interest. *David J. Williams*

Trains crossing

Above: The crew of SR Bulleid Pacific No 34039 *Boscastle* look out from the footplate to observe WR 'Manor' class 4-6-0 No 7820 *Dinmore Manor* entering the down road with the 4.5pm Bishops Lydeard-Minehead train on 1 April 1996. The rebuilt SR 4-6-2 spent about a month based on the WSR in March and April 1996, being hired primarily to take part in the Railway's 'Somerset & Dorset Anniversary Gala'. *Dinmore Manor* worked a total of 11,139 miles in 1996, a record for a steam engine in one season on the WSR, comfortably beating the previous record of 9,522 miles (achieved by GWR 2-6-2T No 4561 in 1990). *Richard Jones*

Bucket and spades

Left: Sporting a very unusual headboard, which reflects its visit to the seaside, English Electric Type 4 (later Class 40) No 40145 starts the climb of Washford Bank, between Blue Anchor and Washford, with an afternoon train from Minehead to Bishops Lydeard in October 1995. No 40145 — which is based on the East Lancs Railway — was one of four ex-BR main line diesel locomotives that were hired to work trains over the 1995 Diesel Gala Weekend. Its appearance in Somerset was the first time a member of the class had traversed the Minehead branch. *David J. Williams*

Hydraulic duo

Left: The impressive pairing of two BR blue-liveried Western Region diesel-hydraulic locomotives — 'Western' No D1035 *Western Yeoman* and 'Hymek' No D7017 — heads the 3.15pm Minehead-Bishops Lydeard service past Blue Anchor's down distant signal on 13 May 1995. Both locomotives are owned and maintained by the Diesel & Electric Preservation Group, and when not in use are normally stabled at the group's base at Williton station. The D&EPG's fleet of locomotives — all of which are types which once saw services on British Railways Western Region — make a very important contribution to the fortunes and success of the WSR as a whole. *Don Bishop*

Black Monkey bridge

Right: One of the two Class 14 0-6-0 diesel-hydraulic locomotives based on the WSR, No D9551, heads an up train over the unusually-named Black Monkey bridge, about half-way along the steep climb from Blue Anchor to Washford, on 12 April 1987. The Class 14s are used on a variety of duties on the WSR, including passenger services, the 'Quantock Belle' dining services and civil engineering trains. A total of 56 Class 14s were built by British Railways, primarily for working short goods trains and for shunting, but the design was obsolete before it ever left the drawing board due to the demise of local freight traffic by the late 1960s. Many of the class were sold on for industrial use, including both No D9551, and its sister locomotive No D9526 (see page 6), which arrived on the WSR in 1981 and 1980 respectively. Both locomotives are painted in the very attractive BR two-tone green livery.
Stuart Trott

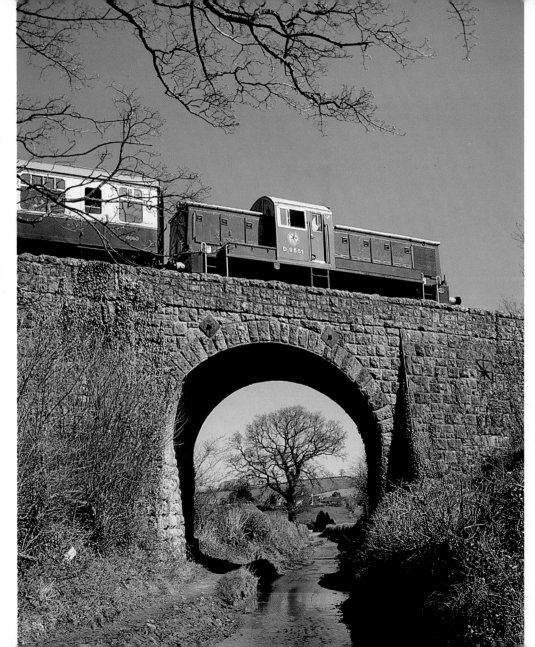

Steam in the landscape

Left: With the hills of Exmoor forming an attractive backdrop, GWR 'Manor' 4-6-0 No 7802 *Bradley Manor* passes over Black Monkey bridge on the climb of Washford bank at the head of the 10.15am Minehead-Bishops Lydeard train on 16 September 1994. After restoration from scrapyard condition, *Bradley Manor* spent an eight-week period working WSR trains, achieving a total mileage of 3,850 in that short period. No 7802 was the first 'Manor' to operate on the 'preserved' WSR, and it proved how ideally suited the class is to the line. The locomotive is based on the Severn Valley Railway, but is also passed to run on Railtrack metals. *David J. Holman*

Gala goods

Left: GWR '2885' Class 2-8-0 No 3822, in wartime black livery (having been built in 1940), heads for Washford on 3 May 1992 with the 7pm Minehead-Bishops Lydeard demonstration goods train, run as part of the railway's Spring Gala Weekend. No 3822 enjoyed a very successful season on the WSR in 1992, but this is the only occasion during its stay when it worked a train for which it was specifically designed. *John P. Robinson*

Dragon's Cross bridge

Right: One of George Jackson Churchward's large
2-8-0T engines, No 4277, coasts down under
Dragon's Cross bridge, between Washford and Blue
Anchor, with a down train in July 1996. The
gradient here is 1 in 65, the steepest on the WSR.
Built in 1920, No 4277 spent the 1996 season
hauling trains on the line, following restoration
from scrapyard condition. Designed for hauling
mineral trains over relatively short distances, the
2-8-0T was well suited to working heavy trains over
the WSR's steep gradients. *Stephen Edge*

Near the summit

Left: Re-creating the British Railways era of the late 1950s, 'Peak' No D120 and Sulzer Type 2 (later Class 25) No D7523 *John F. Kennedy*, both painted in early BR green livery, approach the summit of the incline from Blue Anchor on the approach to Washford station with the 11.15am Minehead-Bishops Lydeard service on 4 May 1996, the first day of the Railway's Spring Gala Weekend. The 'Peak' originally arrived on the WSR in September 1995 to take part in a Diesel Gala event, but has subsequently had its stay extended until 1997. Both locomotives are privately owned, but maintained on the WSR by the Diesel & Electric Preservation Group, whose fleet of locomotives are normally based at Williton. *Don Bishop*

Civil engineers' train

Right: Against a threatening sky, Class 50 No 50149 *Defiance* heads through Washford station with the 11.5am Minehead-Williton demonstration freight train on 28 October 1994 during that year's Autumn Diesel Gala event. This was the locomotive's public début on the WSR, having arrived on the line the previous May after appearing at the Exeter Rail Fair. Originally numbered D449, No 50149 is restored in later BR Railfreight colours, the only member of the once 50-strong class to bear this livery. *Defiance* is now an established member of the 'home' diesel fleet and, when not in service, is also based at Williton. *Richard Jones*

The 'Duke' heads north

Left: BR Standard Class 8P 4-6-2 No 71000 *Duke of Gloucester* makes an impressive sight as it rounds the curve at Kentsford, between Washford and Watchet, with the 10.25am Bishops Lydeard-Minehead train on 28 August 1995. Built in 1954 — the only member of its class — No 71000 was rescued for preservation from a South Wales scrapyard in 1974. Returned to steam in 1986, its restoration is a tremendous achievement. *Duke of Gloucester* was originally meant to be based on the WSR for only a few weeks, stabled in between its main line commitments, but in the end the locomotive spent a very welcome three months on the line. In immaculate condition, and a great credit to its support group, *Duke of Gloucester* ran a total of 1,059 miles on the WSR. During the engine's stay, the maximum permitted axle limit over the whole length of the WSR was formally increased to 23.5 tonnes, thereby enabling the Railway to accept the heaviest locomotives. *Don Bishop*

The down goods

Above: With the tower of St Decuman's church, Watchet, in the distance, GWR '45xx' 2-6-2T No 4561 passes Kentsford on 5 May 1996 heading the 4.40pm demonstration goods from Bishops Lydeard to Minehead. A crossing loop was once located at this point. Owned by the WSR Association, No 4561 is one of the most popular members of the railway's steam fleet. *David J. Holman*

Great Western duo

Left: Both painted in the late GW livery of the Hawksworth era, GWR '2251' class 0-6-0 No 3205 and '64xx' 0-6-0PT No 6412 depart from the single platform at Watchet with a Minehead-bound train during the railway's 1990 Gala Week. Watchet was the first terminus of the original West Somerset Railway, opened in 1862. No 3205 is the only surviving member of a class of 120 locomotives built between 1930 and 1948, and has been a member of the WSR's steam fleet since early 1987. The locomotive has to date run over 21,000 miles on the railway, and re-entered service in 1997 after a heavy overhaul at Minehead. No 6412 has been a regular and popular performer on the line since reopening and, until 1993, had run more miles on the WSR than any other engine. It, too, was welcomed back into service in 1997 after overhaul by its owners, the WSR Association. *Peter Doel*

Passing Watchet docks

Above: Back in the days when Watchet was able to boast a working port, GWR 0-6-0PT No 6412 departs from the station on 28 May 1989 with a late afternoon up train to Bishops Lydeard. The docks — which were the main reason why the railway was built — closed to commercial traffic in 1992. Watchet is the third busiest station on the WSR, though the signalbox and sidings had all gone well before the preservationists took over the line, leaving little evidence of their existence. No 6412 was originally bought straight out of BR service for use on the Dart Valley Railway, but purchased from there by the WSR Association in early 1976.
Peter W. Gray

Big tank power

Left: With the Quantock Hills rising in the background, a well turned out GWR '42xx' 2-8-0T No 4277 coasts downhill past Helwell Bay and approaches Watchet with the 2.10pm Bishops Lydeard-Minehead train on 13 August 1996. This big tank engine — originally built for short distance heavy mineral traffic, such as moving coal from the South Wales pits to the nearby coastal ports — spent the 1996 season working on the WSR, and proved itself easily capable of hauling the line's heaviest trains. During its season in West Somerset, No 4277 ran a total of 5,734 miles. *Richard Jones*

Heading inland

Right: Passengers from Minehead get their last glimpse of the sea at Helwell Bay, on the approach to Doniford Beach Halt, as S&DJR '7F' 2-8-0 No 88 (BR No 53808) heads inland with an up train on 4 April 1994. The station at Doniford was opened in 1988, primarily to serve a nearby holiday camp. The '7F' 2-8-0s were built specifically for work on the steeply graded Somerset & Dorset Joint Railway between Bath and Bournemouth, No 88 being built in 1925. After withdrawal from active service by British Railways in 1964, the locomotive was rescued from a South Wales scrapyard by the Somerset & Dorset Railway Circle (later Trust) and brought to the WSR in January 1976. The S&DRT's headquarters are at Washford station. *Brian Dean*

Approaching Doniford

Right: The wind whips the smoke quickly away from the chimney of BR(W) '5101' class 2-6-2T No 4160 as it heads the 3.55pm train from Bishops Lydeard near Doniford on 4 April 1994. Built by British Railways to a Great Western design at Swindon in 1948, No 4160 was brought to the WSR in 1990 and restored at Minehead, entering service on the line in August 1993. The 'Large Prairie' carries the very attractive early BR lined black livery. *Brian Dean*

Diesel Gala pairing

Left: Two former Western Region diesel-hydraulic locomotives, 'Warship' No D821 *Greyhound* and 'Western' No D1035 *Western Yeoman*, catch the light as they approach Williton station on 29 October 1994 with the 11.25am Minehead-Norton Fitzwarren service, during the railway's Diesel Gala Weekend when some trains ran over the whole 23 miles of the WSR. The 'Western' is a member of the 'home' fleet, whereas *Greyhound* is based on the Severn Valley Railway and visited the line for a short period that autumn to star at the Diesel Gala. It was the first 'Warship' to work in the West Country for 23 years.
Richard Jones

The first of many

Right: Two views showing GWR '4575' class 2-6-2T No 5572 in action on the WSR on 16 April 1987. In the top photograph, the 'Small Prairie' rounds the curve from Doniford with the 2.30pm Minehead-Williton train, whilst the lower view shows No 5572 departing from Williton station with the 3.25pm return working to Minehead. The locomotive spent the latter part of the 1986 season and most of 1987 based on the WSR. It was initially hired at short notice to stand in for GWR 0-6-0PT No 6412, which had failed with a slipped driving wheel tyre, and in doing so became the first 'guest' steam locomotive to be hired by the WSR from elsewhere. Normally based at Didcot Railway Centre, No 5572 worked an estimated total of 9,000 miles in service on the line, the highest mileage of any visiting locomotive. Two other Great Western engines were subsequently hired from Didcot — 2-6-2T No 6106 in 1991 and 1993, and 2-8-0 No 3822 in 1992. *Both: Richard Jones*

Magnificent 'Manor'

Left: The penultimate member of its class, BR(W) 'Manor' 4-6-0 No 7828 *Odney Manor* passes Williton's down advanced starting signal on 14 September 1996 heading the 5.45pm Bishops Lydeard-Minehead train. No 7828 became the second 'Manor' to be used on the 'preserved' WSR, arriving on the line in April 1995. The locomotive has since become an established member of the 'home' fleet. *Odney Manor* is currently receiving a heavy overhaul at Swindon, but will return again to the WSR once this is complete. *Mark Wilkins*

Diesels at Williton

Williton is the home of the 'Williton Traction Group', which is responsible for the operation and maintenance of the bulk of the WSR diesel locomotive fleet.

Top right: English Electric Type 1 (later Class 20) No D8110 rests in the sunshine on 29 October 1993, prior to working trains at the railway's Autumn Diesel Gala. Restored in BR green livery, the locomotive is normally based on the South Devon Railway. On the left is one of the railway's small fleet of diesel multiple-units (a Park Royal two-car set), which are used regularly in the off-peak timetable and on 'relief' workings at other times. *Richard Jones*

Bottom right: An impressive line-up of diesel traction outside the former goods shed at Williton (now used as a workshop) on 26 February 1995. From left to right: Class 08 No 08850, Class 52 No D1035 *Western Yeoman*, Sentinel shunter No 57, and Class 35s Nos D7017 and D7018. With the exception of the Sentinel (which has since been sold and moved elsewhere), all these locomotives have worked passenger trains on the WSR, but in the case of No 08850 this is restricted to one working, on 19 August 1995, when it was sent to rescue No D7018 which had failed whilst working an evening dining train. A new purpose-built shed for the WSR's growing fleet of diesel traction has since been constructed to the right of the existing shed. *Richard Jones*

Williton station

Above: Williton, being approximately 10 miles distant from both Minehead and Bishops Lydeard, is the principal crossing place on the WSR. On 28 October 1994, the 10.15am from Minehead crosses the 10.30am ex-Bishops Lydeard, hauled by 'Western' No D1062 *Western Courier* and 'Hymek' No D7018 respectively. The latter is the second of two 'Hymeks' owned by the Diesel & Electric Preservation Group. *Western Courier* was hired by the railway for use at the 1994 Diesel Gala, where it starred with 'Warship' No D821 *Greyhound*. Both locomotives are normally resident on the Severn Valley Railway. *Richard Jones*

Prairie tank at Castle Hill

Right: In spectacular light, GWR '45xx' 2-6-2T No 4561 passes Castle Hill — one of the most popular photographic locations on the WSR — with the 6pm Minehead to Bishops Lydeard on 3 September 1990. *Brian Dean*

Spring sunshine

Left: With Doniford Stream in the foreground, LMS Class 4F 0-6-0 No 44422 steams past Castle Hill, between Williton and Stogumber, with the 5.40pm Minehead-Bishops Lydeard train on 5 May 1996. The '4F' enjoyed a very successful visit to the WSR in the first half of 1996. *Brian Dean*

S&D local train

Above: BR Standard Class 5 4-6-0 No 73096, running as No 73052, re-creates the era of the Somerset & Dorset line local train in the BR era, as it passes Castle Hill on 13 March 1996 with a special charter train. Castle Hill is one of the most popular photographic locations on the WSR.

No 73096 was another of the four engines hired to participate in the 'Somerset & Dorset Anniversary Gala' in March 1996. Normally resident on the Mid-Hants Railway, it worked WSR trains on just four days, achieving a total mileage of 266. *Don Bishop*

Undisturbed

Left: The local sheep seem unimpressed by the sight and sound of 'Western' diesel-hydraulic No D1010 *Western Campaigner* as it coasts downhill at Woolston Moor on 1 October 1995 with a down train for Minehead. No D1010 is owned and maintained by the Diesel & Electric Preservation Group at Williton, arriving on the WSR in early 1991 having previously been located at Foster Yeoman's Merehead Quarry in Somerset. For many years, No D1010 operated on the WSR as No D1035 *Western Yeoman*, reflecting the name of its previous owners (see page 16), but in 1995 it returned to its true identity as *Western Campaigner*. During its period on the WSR, the 'Western' has already carried three liveries — desert sand, early BR green and late 'all over' BR blue (as shown here). *Glen Batten*

The 'up' parcels

Right: Another BR blue-liveried former Western Region diesel-hydraulic, 'Warship' No D832 *Onslaught*, works a train of parcels vans (the 2.15pm ex-Minehead) at Woolston Moor, on the climb between Williton and Stogumber, on 1 October 1995, during the railway's Diesel Gala. The WSR's diesel events have gained a fine reputation among railway enthusiasts. Following in the footsteps of the only other preserved 'Warship' No D821 *Greyhound* (see page 28), *Onslaught* was one of four visiting locomotives which took part in the 1995 Diesel Gala. The locomotive is based on the East Lancs Railway. *David J. Williams*

Charter goods

Above: LMS 'Black 8' 2-8-0 No 48773 heads a special photographers' charter goods train on 30 April 1993 past Newton, between Williton and Stogumber. This was the first day in service of the '8F' on the WSR. No 48773 achieved a total mileage of 7,688 on the WSR during 1993.
David J. Holman

'Small Prairie' at Stogumber

Right: GWR '45xx' 2-6-2T No 4561 makes a spirited departure from Stogumber heading the 10.15am train from Minehead on 5 September 1991. No 4561 was one of three GWR 'Small Prairie' tanks purchased for use on the WSR from a South Wales scrapyard in 1975. Owned by the WSR Association, the locomotive entered service after restoration in September 1989, and has subsequently proved itself to be a very capable performer, well liked by footplate crews. The station at Stogumber is unique on the WSR in that the platform and main building are on opposite sides of the track to each other. *David J. Holman*

Leigh loop

Left: In glorious late afternoon sunshine, BR(W) '5101' class 2-6-2T No 4160 coasts downhill past the site of Leigh Bridge loop, about a mile south of Stogumber, on 19 October 1995 with the 4pm Bishops Lydeard-Minehead train. Members of the class were used regularly on the branch in GWR and BR days, being ideally suited to the line. Since entering service after restoration in August 1993, No 4160 has run 28,638 miles on the WSR — a creditable achievement. *Tony Whitby*

Bottom left: With 'steam on' for the benefit of the camera, BR Standard Class 4 4-6-0 No 75069 works a charter train formed of various parcels vans at the site of the former loop on 3 May 1994. The locomotive was the principal 'guest' engine in the 1994 season, and actually arrived on the WSR at the head of a railtour, which it worked throughout from Worcester to Minehead, thus creating history as this was the first steam working from Taunton directly onto the WSR for 30 years. *Don Bishop*

Right: No D1041 *Western Prince*, in the admirable maroon livery, became the third 'Western' diesel to operate on the WSR when it visited the line for the 1995 Diesel Gala. The 3.50pm from Norton Fitzwarren to Minehead coasts downhill at Leigh loop on 29 September 1995. *Western Prince*, like No 40145 and No D832 *Onslaught* (see pages 16 and 37), is normally based on the East Lancs Railway at Bury. *Richard Jones*

S&D Gala goods

Left: The days of the '7F'-hauled goods train on the Somerset & Dorset line perfectly re-created. S&DJR '7F' 2-8-0 No 53808 — renumbered as the scrapped No 53806 — coasts downhill on the approaching to Leigh Wood Crossing, between Stogumber and Crowcombe, with the 2.35pm Bishops Lydeard-Minehead goods on 10 March 1996. Having lain in a South Wales scrapyard for several years, the '7F' was restored to working order at Washford and Minehead, entering service on the WSR in the second half of 1987. The locomotive is painted in unlined black livery with the later BR emblem on the tender, the third different livery it has carried since its restoration. *David J. Williams*

By the woods

Right: Amidst beautiful scenery, the image of the West Country branch line train is re-created by GWR '64xx' 0-6-0PT No 6412 heading its four-coach train — the 10.15am from Minehead to Bishops Lydeard — past Leigh Woods on 2 May 1990. Purchased by the WSR Association in late 1975, No 6412 made its WSR debut in service on the railway at Easter 1976 and since then has run over 38,000 miles on the line — a total subsequently exceeded by both the Somerset & Dorset 2-8-0 No 53808 and the GWR 'Small Prairie' No 4561. *Brian Dean*

Double-headers at Roebuck

Top left: The era of the 'Cambrian Coast Express' between Shrewsbury and Aberystwyth in the late 1950s is perfectly recreated in this view of two 'Manor' class 4-6-0s, Nos 7820 *Dinmore Manor* and 7828 *Odney Manor,* as they work a private charter for photographers around the curve past Roebuck Farm on 13 May 1996. The 'Manors' are ideally suited to the WSR. Following purchase from its previous owners in 1984, No 7820 was overhauled from scrapyard condition at the Birmingham Railway Museum, entering WSR service in September 1995. Since then, up to the end of 1996, it has run over 13,000 miles. No 7828 was brought to the line in full working order in 1994 and, like No 7820, is a member of the 'home' fleet. *Don Bishop*

Bottom left: The unusual sight of two Class 50 diesel locomotives in BR Railfreight livery. No 50149 *Defiance* leads No 50117 *Royal Oak* at the head of the 1.50pm Bishops Lydeard-Minehead train on 5 October 1996, during the railway's 'Not the 1996 Diesel Gala' event. *Defiance* was in fact the only Class 50 to carry this livery whilst in service with British Rail, and it has been a popular performer on the WSR since its arrival in May 1994. *Royal Oak* arrived on the line in 1996 and was actually being towed 'dead' on this occasion as its restoration has yet to be completed. It is anticipated that both locomotives will be repainted in their original 'all over' BR blue in 1998, as Nos D449 and D417 respectively. *Richard Jones*

Climbing hard

Above: SR rebuilt Bulleid Pacific No 34039 *Boscastle* — normally based at Loughborough — makes a superb sight as it rounds Roebuck Curve, between Stogumber and Crowcombe, on 10 March 1996 with the 10.50am Minehead-Bishops Lydeard.

Hired specifically to take part in a very successful 'Somerset & Dorset Gala Weekend', *Boscastle* worked a total of 660 miles during its month-long stay on the WSR in early 1996. The operation of No 34039 provided a foretaste of things to come, as

the WSR Association is currently restoring sister engine No 34046 *Braunton* from scrapyard condition at Williton for future use on the line.
David J. Holman

Wartime freight

Left: With the gorse in bloom, S&DJR '7F' 2-8-0 No 88 — one of only two members of the class preserved — heads a wartime freight around Roebuck Curve in the early morning of 8 May 1994. The special train was run as part of a Wartime Weekend organised by the WSR Association to commemorate the 50th anniversary of D-Day. No 88 carried this S&D unlined black livery between the spring of 1992 and early 1996. *David J. Holman*

Minehead bound

Above: The pleasing combination of Class 25 No D7523 *John F. Kennedy* — named after its owner — and Class 45 No D120 passes Stones Wood, on the descent from Crowcombe, with a down train on 4 May 1996. *Glen Batten*

Near Roebuck Crossing

Left: LMS Class 4F 0-6-0 No 44422 — one of 772 locomotives built between 1911 and 1941 — makes good progress up the gradient on the approach to Roebuck Crossing, near Crowcombe, with an up train bound for Bishops Lydeard in March 1996. Normally based on the North Staffordshire Railway, No 44422 spent a very successful period on the WSR between March and June 1996, running a total of 1,863 miles. Its performance on the WSR made an interesting comparison with the GWR Collett 0-6-0, No 3205. *Peter Vile*

Approaching the summit

Right: An impressive study of the S&DJR '7F' 2-8-0 No 88 as it blasts under Crowcombe Bridge, on the approach of the summit of the line at Crowcombe Heathfield station (400ft above sea level), with a special goods charter working for photographers in October 1993. Owned by the Somerset & Dorset Railway Trust — who are based at Washford station — the '7F' is currently out of service awaiting a heavy overhaul, having run almost 50,000 miles between 1987 and 1996. *Mike Goodfield*

Cambrian Coast Express

Left: GWR 'Manor' class 4-6-0 No 7802 *Bradley Manor*, complete with a large 4,000gal tender, 'gets the road' to enter the loop at Crowcombe Heathfield with an up train on 17 September 1994. No 7802 performed admirably during its nine-week stay on the WSR that summer. *Glen Batten*

Smoky arrival

Above: The popular Somerset & Dorset '7F' 2-8-0 No 53808 enters an immaculate Crowcombe Heathfield station — the summit of the line, 400ft above sea level — with the 12 noon train from Minehead to Bishops Lydeard on 20 August 1990. The locomotive is seen bearing the early BR lion-and-wheel emblem on its tender, the livery it carried after returning to service following restoration in 1987. The '7F' has been the mainstay of the WSR steam fleet, achieving a total of 49,303 miles between 1987 and 1996 — more than any other locomotive. No 53808 is now out of service awaiting a heavy overhaul. *Brian Dean*

Class 4 power

Above: BR Class 4 4-6-0 No 75069 drifts into the down platform at Crowcombe Heathfield station on 28 May 1994 with the first train of the day, the 10.25am from Bishops Lydeard. Having been removed by British Railways, the signalling installation at the station was reinstated by the WSR and commissioned the following day. It achieved recognition in the 'National Railway Heritage Awards' in 1996. Normally resident on the Severn Valley line, the Class 4 spent the 1994 season on the WSR, achieving a total mileage of 7,308. It was the second BR Standard locomotive to work on the 'preserved' WSR (after No 92220 *Evening Star* — see page 13). *David J. Holman*

Spring sunshine

Above: With the Quantock Hills just discernible through the trees, 'Hymek' Type 3 (Class 35) diesel-hydraulic No D7017 approaches Nornvis Bridge, near Crowcombe with the 5.40pm Bishops Lydeard-Minehead train on 6 May 1995. The locomotive is one of several locomotives owned or under the care of the Diesel & Electric Preservation Group, based at Williton. No D7017 was in fact the first locomotive preserved by the D&EPG, and the first main line diesel locomotive to arrive on the WSR. As well as running regularly in West Somerset, the 'Hymek' has also made short visits to a number of other preserved railways.
Mike Goodfield

Santa Special

Left: In glorious light, GWR Collett 0-6-0 No 3205 — the only member of its class preserved — passes Nethercott with a Santa Special working from Bishops Lydeard to Crowcombe on 6 December 1992. Such trains are a regular feature of the WSR calendar. This popular locomotive was purchased for preservation directly from British Railways in 1965, and has been a member of the WSR steam fleet since 1987. After working over 21,000 miles, No 3205 was withdrawn for overhaul in 1993, and returned to service in 1997. *Peter Doel*

Nethercott

Above: An idyllic country scene, as BR(W) 'Manor' class 4-6-0 No 7828 *Odney Manor* passes the hamlet of Nethercott, between Crowcombe Heathfield and Bishops Lydeard, with a train bound for Minehead on 4 May 1996. No 7828 has to date run 11,213 miles on the WSR. *Glen Batten*

Midsummer steam

Left: Amidst the beautiful Quantock Hills, the Great Western double-headed combination of 'City' class 4-4-0 No *3440 City of Truro* and '2251' class 0-6-0 No 3205 approach Combe Florey, climbing towards Crowcombe, with the 3.55pm Bishops Lydeard-Minehead service on 27 July 1992. *City of Truro* spent a very successful few weeks working on the WSR that summer, on loan from the National Railway Museum at York. No 3205 is an established member of the 'home' fleet. *Brian Dean*

'Growlers'

There have to date been two occasions on which English Electric Type 3 (later Class 37) diesel-electric locomotives — nicknamed 'Growlers' by enthusiasts — have worked passenger trains on the WSR.

Top right: In less than ideal weather conditions, 'Transrail'-liveried Class 37 No 37407 *Blackpool Tower* approaches Eastcombe cutting from the north with the return leg of 'The Quantock Quester' railtour on 11 March 1995, which it worked throughout between Cardiff and Minehead, thus achieving a total mileage of just 46 on the WSR! *Richard Jones*

Bottom right: In BR Railfreight grey livery, No 37699 approaches Eastcombe cutting from the south with the 9.40am Bishops Lydeard-Minehead working on 31 October 1992 — the first BR diesel-worked passenger train to Minehead for 21 years — during that year's Autumn Diesel Gala. The locomotive spent just two days working passenger trains on the WSR. *Don Bishop*

Auto train

Left: GWR '14xx' 0-4-2T No 1450, propelling 'blood-and-custard'-liveried trailer No W228W, positively glows in the sunshine as it passes a stubble field at Watersmeet with the 4.45pm auto train from Bishops Lydeard to Minehead on 15 September 1996, the last day of a very successful Autumn Gala Weekend. Auto trains were introduced by the Great Western on branch lines to avoid the locomotive having to run round its train. The auto trailer is normally based on the South Devon Railway; No 1450 was based on the WSR between September 1996 and January 1997. *Mark Wilkins*

Steam to spare

Right: With the Blackdown Hills forming the backdrop, GWR '2884' class 2-8-0 No 3822 climbs away from Bishops Lydeard and passes over Watersmeet Bridge with a train for Minehead on 22 August 1992. This 'heavy freight' locomotive was the principal 'guest' engine for the 1992 season, being hired from Didcot Railway Centre, and it worked a total of 6,714 miles on the WSR. During its period on the line, No 3822 successfully hauled a train of 19 coaches from Minehead to Bishops Lydeard — then a preservation record. The 2-8-0 proved ideally suited to the line, and another member of the class — No 3850 — is currently being restored at Minehead for use on the branch. *Brian Dean*

GW 'Large Prairies'

The Great Western 'Large Prairie' tank engines were used regularly on the Minehead branch from the 1930s until the end of steam, allocated to Taunton shed. To date, two examples of these large 2-6-2 tanks have operated on the 'preserved' WSR.

Far left: On a gloriously sunny morning, after overnight frost, '5101' class 2-6-2T No 4160 makes a spectacular sight as it approaches Whisky Trail Crossing, near Bishops Lydeard, whilst performing a run past for the cameras during a photographers' charter event on 20 November 1993. No 4160 is a regular member of the 'home' fleet. *Bob Webster*

Near left: GWR '61xx' class 2-6-2T No 6106 departs from Bishops Lydeard with the 3.55pm train to Minehead on 3 May 1993, during the locomotive's second visit to the WSR. This 'Large Prairie' has worked 7,097 miles over its two visits to the line. *Don Bishop*

Approaching Lydeard

Top right: GWR '45xx' 2-6-2T No 4561 approaches Bishops Lydeard with a demonstration goods train from Minehead in May 1996. The locomotive has also been hired out to other preserved lines, working on five different railways in 1996. *David J. Williams*

Bottom right: BR Class 07 diesel shunter No D2994 coasts into Bishops Lydeard station with an engineers' train in July 1981. Whilst used primarily for shunting and works trains on the WSR, No D2994 was used occasionally on passenger trains in the 1980s, usually when nothing else was available! It has now left the WSR for pastures new. *Stephen Edge*

The country station

Left: GWR '14xx' 0-4-2T No 1450 rests with its auto trailer in the down platform at Bishops Lydeard in September 1996. The 'auto tank' worked a total of 649 miles whilst based on the WSR. *David J. Williams*

Awaiting passengers

Above: The 'old faithful' Great Western 2-6-2T No 4561 waits at Bishops Lydeard prior to taking out the 10.40am train to Minehead on 31 December 1994. The 'Small Prairie' was rescued for use on the WSR in 1976 and, after restoration from scrapyard condition at Minehead, it entered service on the line in September 1989. Since then, up to the end of 1996, No 4561 has achieved a total mileage of 38,660 on the WSR. *David J. Holman*

Pure gold

Left: Early morning at Bishops Lydeard. In tremendous lighting conditions, BR(W) '5101' class 2-6-2T No 4160 prepares to take water from the tower at the start of its day's work on 20 November 1993. The BR black-liveried 'Large Prairie' tank entered service on the WSR in August 1993, and has quickly established itself as a popular and reliable locomotive, ideally suited to the line. *David J. Williams*